MW01046037

To Robert

in good
neighbourhood

Marguerite
Andersen

May 8, 2005

ESSENTIAL POETS SERIES 114

Guernica Editions Inc. acknowledges the support of
The Canada Council for the Arts.
Guernica Editions Inc. acknowledges the support of
the Ontario Arts Council.
Guernica Editions Inc. acknowledges the financial support of
the Government of Canada through the Book Publishing Industry Development
Program (BPIDP).
Guernica Editions Inc. acknowledges the Government of Ontario through the Ontario
Media Development Corporation's Ontario Book Initiative.

MARGUERITE ANDERSEN

DREAMING OUR SPACE

TRANSLATED BY THE AUTHOR
AND ANTONIO D'ALFONSO

GUERNICA

TORONTO·BUFFALO·CHICAGO·LANCASTER (U.K.)

2003

Original title: *L'autrement pareille*.
Published by Prise de Parole (Sudbury) in 1984.

Antonio D'Alfonso, editor.
Guernica Editions Inc.
P.O. Box 117, Station P, Toronto (ON), Canada M5S 2S6
2250 Military Road, Tonawanda, N.Y. 14150-6000 U.S.A.

Distributors:
University of Toronto Press Distribution,
5201 Dufferin Street, Toronto, (ON), Canada M3H 5T8

Gazelle Book Services, Falcon House, Queen Square, Lancaster LA1 1RN U.K.

Independent Publishers Group,
814 N. Franklin Street, Chicago, Il. 60610 U.S.A.

First edition.
Printed in Canada.
Legal Deposit – First Quarter
National Library of Canada
Library of Congress Catalog Card Number: 2002113558

National Library of Canada Cataloguing in Publication
Andersen, Marguerite
[Autrement pareille. English]
Dreaming our space / Marguerite Andersen, author ;
Antonio D'Alfonso, translator.
(Essential poets series ; 114)
Poems.
Translation of: L'autrement pareille.
ISBN 1-55071-152-0
1. Prose poems, Canadian (French). I. D'Alfonso, Antonio II. Title.
III. Title: Autrement pareille. English. IV. Series.
PS8551.N297A9813 2002   C843.54   C2002-904867-2
PQ3919.2.A55A9813 2002

CONTENTS

NOTE

First published as *L'autrement pareille* (Prise de parole, Sudbury, 1984). The revised English version is the result of a collaboration between myself and Antonio D'Alfonso, whose vision and energy brought the text to its completion.

A warm thank you to Daniel Sloate for his editorial suggestions.

DREAMING OUR SPACE

My life depends on hers.
George Sand
(speaking of her granddaughter Aurore,
in a letter to Gustave Flaubert,
dated August 31, 1872)

Passages. Written at a time when the once so indispensable mother became dispensable. Daughter in flight. Myself in pain. Terrible pain. Tears. Anger.

Escape to the land of sheltered, childhood days. To my mother's house, my mother deceased yet still very present.

Later the escape into work and the analysis of writings by Nicole Brossard who, in *Lovhers,* nullified the womb for us all.

Distance, appeasement, letters. Need for friendship. We ask in unison: Can there be a new definition for *mother?* There must be.

Hush, my sweet daughter. Don't be scared. No, I will not tell you what happened. I will spare you the details, the story. I will speak of things more powerful, obscure, things hidden that swiftly swirl, seethe, spin, strain, things that remind me of you in your world, remind me of the others in theirs.

No, I will not cry out to you for help. Here, in this house, with my self, speaking quietly, softly, I will follow the long and winding path that leads to the top of the mountain. Words that march in straight lines are obstacles. What other choice? I will try to turn my words upside down, topsy-turvy, pushing them up to you, my only centre, and for the sake of caring and love, joy and tenderness, offer my words to others.

I want these words to go to the deeper reaches of you which I can't touch. My hands, my lips, to move up your body, from the bottom of this page to the loftiest places, caressing you, giving you pleasure, telling you

of the snow in my silent garden, quiet under the bare blue sky. Trees stand firm, the bushes are still in their nakedness. Should I lie down in the cold drift of white? Listen. The furnace sings. I stay inside. Separated from the cold, I am dreaming behind a window, in this gentle house.

Imaginary home, sand castle, water, air, open doors, a space to go to and leave behind, calm dissension. From the chimney, signals of life and warmth. The kettle calls. The mango tea, a gift from you, is brewing. Magic potion. I see images: lines of words like the strands of a girl's hair braided by her mother.

On my desk, my glasses. Reflected in them, the window curtain, my hand following the pen from the beginning to the end of a line.

Nothing else is moving. Not in this room. Not in the twin images reflected in the lenses. Not in the large old mirror where the scene is held.

Like magic, the tip of my pen traces words for me. This is the only way I can prevent the moment from filling itself with you. I want to remain neutral by concentrating on what is before me and by encapsulating the complex nature of simple things, the bonding between women.

Desire sets you sailing without direction. To a distant island that I with my myopic eyes cannot see. You fill me with anguish. Possessive, loving anguish. I fear the distancing, *die Verfremdung*. How will I survive? Why must you become a foreign body? Strangely possessive, you want me to be the immovable pier, the compass needle turning always toward you, a harbour forever open but without ties. This I cannot be.

I'm insured. Insured against theft, fire, illness. I am insured for mental or physical disability. I am insured against toothaches and forgetfulness. The company is willing to compensate for everything. My funeral too is taken care of. But there is no insurance against melancholy. No insurance against despair. None.

Muscles are tense. Jaws clenched. I tremble in fear. The tenacious mind searches for the outcome of a life that has hardly begun, a path that has not yet been taken. May your journey be less tortuous than mine.

My thoughts, entangled like the colourful yarns of a complex knitting, drop into the terrifying depths of dark despair.

I have to stop. Pause. Stop thinking. Feel no agitation, no stress. Neither hear, nor see, nor touch. Smell nothing, taste nothing. Pause. Stop. Cease trying to understand. Imagine the unimaginable. Such is my task. Impossible.

Interval for consonants: Knots, small stitches entwined, knit, purl, and repeat, a rhythm perfected. I never quarrel with my love born under the African sun, she has no need for swaddling clothes. I am knitting a sleeveless white sweater. With thick needles, I create holes through which the soft air will blow onto your even softer skin.

Skin of my skin, my sweet one, my world, you and I, web linking mother and daughter. Silver-threaded coat of letters. Weightless chains. Garlands along which we dance, you first, then me.

Interval.
A knitting to pursue.

No, you don't give me joy.
I do not depend on you
For my pleasure.
but life is better with you,
sleep less light.

Solitary. Soliloquy. Being silent, alone, as she becomes the Other for an unspecified length of time, perhaps forever, from which we will emerge dead or alive, who can tell? She wants to be herself, and rightly so. She clearly turns me into the object of my own folly. Desire is clearly ferocious in her, and immediately nullifies me in my consciousness. More and more I pull away, efface myself, become minimal. A mini-mother reduced to the smallest possible proportions by a perfectly loving daughter.

Demented Demeter, I err, frightened, within the labyrinth. The entanglement is total, every path is without exit. I long for you in the centre. I wait for you. I cannot see you. Where does the spiral begin? Where is Ariadne, she who will lead me out of here? I pursue her as she runs through the complex design. I persist. Unqualified, I search with all of my body for a lost daughter. I shred the blue and green coat of love, shreds I cannot turn into flowers. *Demented Demeter*. I want to believe in the tender union of mother and daughter.

Not to die
Not one
Not the other.

Impatient, the young hand can with one smooth immediately forgotten gesture wave away the hurt, the unwelcome weight.

Suddenly I am soothed, and I touch you lovingly. Yes, I dare touch my pink neurosis. My gentle hand shall bring forth the gentle answer I am waiting for. Your silent lips will soon offer me a smile, just as I will once and for all abandon the prison language masters imposed on us and replace it with the language of women who will refuse to imprison one another.

Female minds, passion builders who dispense with orders and commands, hollow words that serve no purpose. We invent new words, our own words, the non-words of delirium calling for non-reason and pleasure.

We shall rest at last. Embrace. In clarity and lucidity. In love, most certainly in love. Yes.

The Berber at her vertical loom weaves a shawl of blue wool. Gestures, smiles, words, a short encounter, an exchange of object and money between craftswoman and tourist. The story resembles ours, my love. We leave one another, half-filled with memories of a woman who wove the backdrop of life for us. Mother. Yours, mine. Do we want these memories to come into focus? Perhaps during those days of inner house-cleaning? The more I wash the shawl that now covers my desk, the more its white geometric patterns become visible.

Disaster time again. Tears without end. The beloved leaves unable to say farewell. Mother of vinegar, I want to cry a sea of joy tears, open wide the doors I myself opened twenty years ago. Leave me, I beg you.

All my muscles become tense. Childbirth happens readily. Adult-birth brings deeper pain. Why use forceps this time around? The tear is unending. The umbilical cord tightens around my neck. In my throat there is no cry, my breathing is imperceptible. If I stop to move, will I have the strength to be a thousand times stronger? Motionless, will I become insensitive? Desensitized? Cold? Will my tears harden into ice?

Monstrous mother, I delve into dreams of spectacular desire. I long for my swallow of fire, miss her coming and going. I am a fragmented female. Worn out. Shattered. I must put an end to my dream of mater-filial belonging. Cut off these hands which too wildly long for her. Sever my thoughts, my words. Open my veins and pour my blood into the failing world . . .

If you do it, you said
in your carefree way,
do it well.
As if I had done things badly before.
Be sure, you said.
As if I never had been.
You left.
The other, my son,
calls, reassures me, reminds me
of what remains to be done.
Still another, the doctor, prescribes
magic pills
that prevent me from seeing clearly.
I drown
in your departure
in his good-bye,
in these vain remedies.
The door closes
seemingly forever.
A wounded
wreck,
I drift
at large.
Unmasked.

The tree is a possibility, yet fallible. Awkward, because of the old woman next door in her garden, children running left and right. How to perform without hurting another person? The reliable car of safe journeys . . . Where is the deep ravine that will reduce infirmity to nothingness? Fear prevents me from taking action.

Drugs, stones and the long walk into the river, cold and black. Oh, to have Virginia's strength, her hopelessness. And not this hope, this waiting for a change, an obscure Godot.

Fear. Always. Not knowing.

To experience the ultimate birth. The premature child placed in the sterile incubator. The empty belly. Waiting to hold her, protect her, rock her with love. To sing to her.

Waiting for her in the silenced home from which she escaped. To be able to welcome her and make her feel safe. To celebrate her.

Waiting in front of the dilapidated house she chose for shelter – a gazelle with limpid eyes. The porch crumbles under the weight of its occupants. Obscene scene.

I am hurting, without power before the apparent catastrophe. Let her go, they say. Will she have the strength to surface? When? Waiting: compulsive, repetitive, painful. The pleasure principle collapsing, experience means nothing. Failure does not elucidate. Fervent desire confirms breakdown and helplessness.

The tormented self.

And once again we begin the repetitive discourse. I miss you. I conjure you. I imagine your presence. You decline to be as I see you. Between us an empty space we try to fill with words, glances, gestures. Affection. You give me your timetable, marked in red, yellow and green. This should enable me to follow you from afar, without losing myself. I mislay the sheet of paper, choose exclusion over certitude. It's my turn to deny the silence of these endless hours.

Yes, Sarah Derive Stein was a woman and you carry her with you in your personal notes.
Nicole Brossard, *Picture Theory*

Once more I undertake the pilgrimage across the ocean to my homeland. To the one who protected me in my childhood. Canada fades behind me. I am flying into the clear morning light.

I choose to return to discipline, the tempered countenance of my origins. I enter the orderly torpor of the German household where my obedient sister follows the instructions of her husband, a civil servant. No letting go, a pulling together of the self at all times. Under my wrists the cold beauty of our parents' marble dining-table. No leaning on elbows. I speak quietly, without excitement. I do not whittle away the silence, I am simply thinking of my deceased mother. Mother by the sea. The Baltic Sea. Mother. Let us be silent. This is my quest.

This is a time for recollection. I walk through the spacious house where every piece of furniture, every single silver spoon, every wooden spoon, every porcelain cup, every clothes peg, every particle of air touched by the tall, beautiful woman comes alive for me. My mother. I search for her. I want to receive from her the help I do not dare ask from you. I wish I could speak to her about you, my reality, more real than anything else. I long to hear her gentle words. Once upon a time, I refused to help her and only wanted to leave. Left as you are leaving me.

The colour white dominates my image of her. I hide my face in the old kitchen towel she used to hang next to the sink. I weep. Listen. When I turn to her, my thoughts are crowded with sheets and napkins, pillow-cases and duvet covers, in damask, cotton and percale. My mother, gentle guardian of starched treasures, looks at me across a wasteland of white. White like the winter whiteness that covers the country I chose to live in.

Pale mother, mother nonetheless. I quietly unlock the trunk that contains the table linen. I recognize the embroidered tablecloth that at times she would place over the marble table. From its pale flowers rises a pale image.

Her calm silhouette against the thin, powder-blue curtains. She rests her arms on the top of her desk. A woman's desk, made of inlaid mahogany. She removes the lid from the painted porcelain inkwell. She takes her pen from the small and heavy crystal jar filled with green glass beads, dips the pen into the inkwell. She begins to write. Household accounts, not love letters.

The daughter marvels at the way her mother juggles such figures. She is waiting quietly for her to be free. The child understands that in the end one must be capable of being alone. A lesson learned. Each one of us is fundamentally linked to the other and yet totally alone.

She is ashes. You are vitality,
I too,
despairing of my will to live,
shall slowly
burn
to ashes.

A lesson learned but not by heart.

In a dream which I did not dream, the beautiful sideboard has been disemboweled. My mother's entrails are knives, forks, spoons. Salt has spilled out of the salt-cellars. The plates are empty. The cups dry. My mother calls out, "Dinner is ready!" I am alone and the chairs have tipped over. Where am I to sit? Where is my place in this incredible disorder? I try to make sense of it all. I am tired of standing on my feet. No one, however, offers me a seat. My mother has disappeared.

My purpose must remain a secret. It does not behoove a person of my age to clamour for her mother. Didn't I at a much younger age rid myself of her? Nobody here would understand my longing for her and so I do not reveal it. I glance furtively at the embroidered cushion she used to tuck behind her back. I dream about her fingers carefully rearranging the porcelain cherubs in the glass cabinet . . . I hear voices. The World Soccer Championship dances over the television screen. Is Germany winning? Champagne bubbles in glasses. I smile. My mother is at my side and nobody knows it.

Velvet night. Summer night. I am unable to sleep. Downstairs, on the terrace, a hedgehog drinks its milk, pushing the saucer with its snout until it slams against the stones. My likeness is sleeping. Seven thousand kilometres away. What does she hear?

Naked, I write.

They say you ran away from home when you were eighteen. They say your parents beat you. You returned three days later. I would have liked to spend those three days with you.

They say you married my father in order to escape.
I would have liked to escape with you.
They say you had two lovers.
I would have wanted to be the third.
In my imagination I am.

Who was she?

A woman defeated by her country. Defeated by history. A handsome and knowledgeable father. A mother ashamed of her own body. A husband forever lecturing. A world of war.

A housewife. Defeated again. Kitchen towels. Doilies. Sterling cutlery. White porcelain. A marble table.

In her dream, the Baltic Sea surrounds her and her three daughters. She imagines life with them on the Women's Island. A Thule where all are faithful, where cups measure the inexhaustible.

A dream only. The three daughters disperse across the continents, their far away realities.

Finally, she was defeated by her body. A body paralyzed, annihilated in all expression of desire. Death in darkness. She passed away, they say. They repeat it.

But I carry her with me indomitably alive, yes, in my personal notes.

Five o'clock. The sleepless night ends with a chorus of birds chanting in the trees. This, too, is Germany. The beautiful, the gentle, the musical. The Germany that, like the other, will never be forgotten.

A poisonous contradiction.

Suddenly a feeling of paralysis. Total weakness. Is it this country, Mother? I cannot move. I realize I did well to flee Germany where you died searching in vain for air, unable to fulfil your longing to escape. I, too, am choking. But one thing is certain: She who resembles us will not accept such silencing, will not be detained. Her ribcage will not suffer the straightjacket imposed on you and me. She will be free where we followed orders. Free of discipline and full of folly. Free and joyous. And I must learn not to fear for her.

I am leaving. I return to my country, with its straight roads and vast spaces. That is where I live, like you, and different. I close the doors of Germany behind me. Shake off its weight. *Die Unfreiheit*. Un-freedom. Word invented by some German philosopher. Paradoxical prefix now lost. This is what you wished for me.

Let me hurry. Be quick. Joyfully grasp whatever is left here of my mother. Take it with me. I cannot live in a country where all doors are kept shut, and exuberance is considered suspect, fantasy prohibited.

Oh joy, it is done: I have absorbed my mother. Baltic Mother. Never again will she be dead, *Martha Joy,* you live in me. I carry you in me.

Joy to know you wanted me to leave and live. You orchestrated my escape, helped me get away from under the weight of the iron cross discipline. Joy, joy, joy. No more need for pilgrimages. I did not desert my mother. Her source and strength are in me. I am a brook that links me to her, elsewhere better than here.

The wind in the shady garden gently lifts the sheets of my manuscript, as if to disperse them. Filled with new energy, my hand catches the pages in their flight. I place them in the black and green folder I bought on rue Saint-André des Arts, in Paris. Thin black ribbons safely tied retain what is precious to me: the need to write, to preserve and to arrest without interrupting the movement of the wind, of my thoughts.

Different waters. Divided.

What is the taste of maternal waters? Would they quench thirst? Such waters sprang from her body, from mine. I want to swim in them without fear of drowning. Share the resplendent stream with all women. We shall delight in floating weightlessly, swimming in felicitous seas.

The airport.

The thick glass pane. And you behind it.

Your glorious smile, short hair, expressive face.

I sense your impatience. I too am impatient, as when I waited to see the school doors open and you running toward me.

My eagerness today is similar to what it was. The same? It is what I remember.

Desire is.

Here I am,
alone, centred in myself
My application to use
the library of a foreign university
where I have come
to remove myself from you
asks for my

PARENTS' ADDRESS

What to answer? Heaven, paradise, hell, nothingness,
manuscript, memory?

No one asks for the address of
my beloved
No one holds her accountable
for me
as they were until their death

Here I am alone
solely responsible
able carrier of the self
except in those horrible moments
when dereliction becomes painfully acute.

Locked into mute, impotent impatience, my body slouches silently. My lips don't move. Tongue held back tightly. Eyes darkened by the mountains around Grenoble behind which lie infinite horizons I can no longer imagine. My ears are attentive to nothing. Under the weight of solitude my hair is heavy and tense with pain. Abstraction alone continues to form words. Writing. Reading. Most often works by other women who carry me as far as I must go. Thought, perception, emotion travelling toward the invisible object of desire.

I am in a space
whose existence, possibility, ugliness
I never suspected
Concentrated abomination
expanding
grey concrete
black graffiti

*Snit / Prick / Cunt / Death to the Bastards / Your Mother
the Whore / No Fun*

Thousands and thousands of apartments
One like the other

VILLENEUVE

At a distance the snowy Alps
Whiteness unalterable inaccessible
I am locked in the greyness
of the new city
and my neurasthenia
This is the off-season

With you
I had become accustomed to evocative addresses
Place des Vosges
Bourg-la-Reine
Bellevue
but today
here I am at the Galeries de l'Arlequin
laughable residence
of seventeen thousand immigrants
including me.
I research
the structure of imaginary realms
at an institute called C.R.I.
And I cry.
I scream my pain
across the huge expanse
of the Hyper-Marché du Carrefour
with its sixty-three cashiers
all taught to know the price of everything
including death.

C.R.I. = L'Institut de Recherche sur l'Imaginaire, Université de Grenoble.

Soundless solitude encloses me. My sole support the folds of a shroud. I thought I was stronger. I fail. *Ma fille*, come to my assistance.

Yet I stand back, refrain from saying too much. Embarrassment. Shame. Mother . . . Daughter . . . People turn away, and want to hear something less trivial, less real. I blush. Mother. Daughter. Is she crazy? Does she not know that cords must be cut? Childish. Motherish. Gibberish. Tears well up. Mother. Daughter. Love. Sickly illusion. Unhealthy attachment. But why not? Our love brought out into the open? It is not possible that it is not possible.

Here I am, on the tenth floor of this monstrous building – a glass and concrete coffin. Suicide's spectre smiles at me across the balcony railing. I dare not step forward. It's a subtle smile. An invitation to risk the definite descent into death, oblivion spiralling down the curved path. I stand still, frightened.

I live without life. *Like in a book on American architecture which, read attentively, would provoke panic in worn-out bodies.* Once again, Nicole expresses for me what my eyes sense in the haunted city.

Perpetual motion. Slow motion. The inner cinematographer projects sunny images of things past onto the screen of my closed eyes. Remembrance. The future remains uniformly grey, constant rain on white cloth.

I wish to rid myself of this acrid taste in my mouth, the sweat around my ankles. To find the courage to face hope, and stop erasing words that speak my dream of a world where everything is possible. Happiness, without failure or obstacle. Permanent well-being.

And you heard me. You call. Distance diminishes. Your voice pulls me from foolish lethargy. Closeness bridges gaps. Mother. Daughter. Friendship. A cup still far removed, hard to reach, lift, drink from. We sense it from afar. I proclaim it, jubilant, oblivious of my suffering. Adult birth has been achieved. For the second time, I have given birth, this time as a gesture of freedom.

It is snowing today. Tiny snowflakes dissolve, one after the other, before they reach the ground. Words calmly fall on virgin paper. Progress. Rhythm. What was there to be feared? I find satisfaction by moving toward the unknown.

Sometimes, I travel on roads I had travelled with you, and memory awakens. But more and more often I tend to choose those roads that neither you nor I have taken. I move forward. Will you check on me for fear that I might get lost? Or will you trust my sense of direction as you did when you were little and we were travelling together? Which do I want? What remains hidden beneath these ill-formulated questions? Contradiction, ambivalence, tunnel to go through without any lamp. Rain over the lake. A policeman regulates traffic. A beautiful inn beckons. I want to stop, sit on its porch, rest my gaze on the large flower boxes. But it seems more urgent to reduce distances and to take a rapid train without crossing the rails at the station. As did my grandmother who, when called to order, simply responded: "Young man, do you not know who I am?"

To possess her quiet self-knowledge.

Clear morning on a rainy spring day. *Emotion is the dream all women think.* I reflect on this sentence. Internalize it. Quote it in public. It frees me of my shame, clears me of my hesitation. Lucid. It assembles three impelling forces that I had learned to believe incompatible.

Balance shooting into vertigo.

Will you laugh at me for hanging on to the old belief that says that books, sounds and images permit us to fill up solitude? Partially at least? I write. I read. I feel well. The radio brings me Fischer-Dieskau singing Schubert. Men in my nun's cell? For the sound. Summoned by me. Women are with me for good. Without women, I would not be. Virginia Woolf, Clara Schumann, Käthe Kollwitz, Simone de Beauvoir, Mary Daly, Adrienne Rich and, closer to home, Freda Guttman, Mary Meigs, Marie-Claire Blais, Madeleine Gagnon, Nicole Brossard, Louky Bersianik. Eyes and voices. Images and books. The collective work of women. For you, for me. My likeness, my reality. For you who dance across my pages, white or covered with words. You, my marvellous diversion.

Today, a void. No images. No words. No music. Only inner and outer torments intensely confounded.

And then, a miracle. In the mailbox, a card. Botticelli's *Primavera. Particolare:* Head of youth, flowers between lips. Amazon face. Impetuous strength. You. My sweet, my friend I have never lost. My adventuress. You. Writing to me in your clear handwriting without curlicues. Studious girl, you tell me of things you want to learn, courses you intend to take. Don't you need to fly some more? Carry flowers between your lips? Fear not. Nothing will reopen the patriarchal wounds so recently cauterized if we nurse the intimate bonds of revolution.

A conference takes me to Venice. A languid bus ride slowed down by striking workers marching on the throughway. Traffic jams. Factories. Garbage dumps. Wheat fields conquered by poppies. Red flags, grey rain. Borjanka, Yugoslav lecturer, her pink umbrella. The lagoon, a few boats.

I feel no haste. Others voice discontent. Borjanka steps out to pee, hides behind the parapet while I hold her flower-like umbrella. The driver laughs, waits.

Slowly, we approach the magic city. Will I die in this fluid town where time has ceased?

A bus advertises:
Esso 766 Highlights of Europe Liebhofers Reisen.

We advance. We approach the city of dreams.
"Intellectual honesty," a voice says behind me.
Children on the road in rain-soaked red running shoes.
Mosquitoes on the windows of the bus. "Without bite,"
says the voice.
The children wave.

VENEZIA.

Germans in their car from Bochum. A fair-headed
Dutchman. His wife.

Join the National Holiday-makers.

Slowly we approach Venice, longingly. Like you and
me, my likeness, my reality, we are getting close. But
must you be with me? Everywhere?
Leave me alone, please, here, now.
EXCITEMENT JOY DELIRIUM

Renaissance in marvellous fluidity.

I didn't think I could survive nine months without see-
ing you, touching you. Ten times twenty-eight days.
Writing letters. Reading letters. From time to time a
phone call. Transatlantic echo. Your words reach me
with a delay of fractions of seconds. Mine seem to run
toward you. Twenty-eight days, a month, a moon ten
times. Both of us timed, nine months of waiting.

It is done. No more dependency. I define myself Other.
Lighter, but always perfectly loving.

The jasmine's perfume rises
my painter friend puts a weeping willow
into the window of Spring
which a swallow, so they say, cannot open.
The jasmine's perfume rises and I return home
to my likeness, my reality.
The jasmine's perfume rises
hug me.
The white thought
dreams its emotion
the jasmine's perfume rises.

Always this tremendous joy at the first contact
repeating *ad infinitum*
the brilliant moment of entering the world.

FINALE AND PRELUDE

Capsules in orbit. Each independent at its core.
Nicole Brossard, *French Kiss*

For a long time I thought we would need a separator. (An instrument, the dictionary explains, to separate elements, water and vapour for instance.) But in fact we are inseparable. Water and vapour. You stay within me. I within you. Forgetting the presence, the absence of the other. You did not want a manly separator who with his force might have taken you who knows where. You chose to remain in the realm of women, on this imaginary island where we are so close, so similar, so intimate. At the risk of hurting each other.

Touch me, gently, again.

The inadmissible lived openly. In front of others. Mothers, daughters in love. Marvellous spectacle.

Unreality I

This winter,
For a short moment
I met the perturbing pater.
Bitterness, he said, and the word
echoed endlessly
in all directions, as far as the eye could go.
Bitter you
bittersweet mother
MOTHER horrendous
His paternal perception appears pernicious
Pater, patriarch, patronizing patron
facetious father
faceless faitor
fastidious patchocke
padclinking padre
pedantic perforator
perilous palterer . . .
My sweet reality, laugh with me.

Unreality II

The anecdote, as told by the defeated patriarch, would have been laughable without the subjacent violence, always threatening eruption.

It was me, he said, who made you what you are, my real one. My strength. Forced you to be different. Accused of omnipotence, I seem cause of everything. Of evil.

Which evil did he mean? The badly turned-out girl whom I love? The woman who refuses to dance to the sound of the male instrument? Her energy he wishes to ignore?

My likeness, my reality, my determined strong daughter. Dance as you please. Don't stop here. I too have thrown overboard the patriarchal ballast of my schooldays and former life. Today, I am different.

I want to release my subconscious. Take it for a walk, and air it out. Replace its shiny patent leather pumps with a pair of sandals. Turn it upside down. Let it dance on its hands. Let its deepest folds face the sun.

Let it become visible.
For me. For you. For others.
Let it be clear:
I am no longer what I once was.

Joyfully, we cement our new alliance with mutual feelings of coming-going-remaining. Slow-drying mortar with neither steel girders nor aggravation. Unreinforced concrete, except for those tender feelings we place in it. Overflowing with desire, we celebrate harmony.

Harmony. I want to engrave this word in stone. Inscribe it in letters of secrecy. Discreetly enabling us to meet life. Our lives. Past, future and present. Martha's daughter and Martha's mother, Martha myself. Three times. Each lost without the other. But free of all restraint. Free to fly in entirely different directions.

I distance myself without slipping into the gray cloak of indifference. I cut the cloak into pieces. Into a thousands strips of multicoloured banners with which to decorate the joyous island, our cities and bodies in celebration. Light, colourful daughter, the same and other. We do not fear ghosts. We no longer descend into torment.

I accept melancholy for what it is: an ineffaceable characteristic of the self. Joyfully, I live with melancholy.

Melajoy, a word to invent.

My good, my most beautiful, my most amiable, most perfectly beloved, here I am joyously pleasing my heart, alone in my room, peacefully writing to you . . . I do not know in which mood you shall be when reading this letter. Perchance it will arrive at an unfortunate time and will not be read in the spirit in which it was written. I know no remedy to this, but my letter helps me to rest, at present; that is all I ask . . . I do not know how not to be with you . . . My daughter, love me always, your friendship is my soul . . . I swear and testify that I have never looked at you with indifference . . . never without joy or without tenderness . . . Some people try to make me believe that my excessive affection bothers you . . . I do not know, my dear, whether that is so, but I don't believe I was ever burdening you . . . I heard a thousand nightingales sing: I thought of those you hear from your balcony . . . I marvel how vivaciously I write to you and how I hate writing to the rest of the world. And, putting this on paper, I find nothing less tender than what I am saying: What? I love writing to you? It means that I love your absence, my daughter, and that is abominable.

Mme de Sévigné (1646-1696),
writing to her daughter, Mme de Grignan

Reality interferes, and brings back inevitable doubt. Badly, madly man-made world. Diving head first into utopia is one solution. Believing that menstrual blood can peacefully and lovingly cleanse the earth soaked with the blood of male violence.

My reality, my likeness, what to do? I am certain circles can be other than vicious. I know so. I want to grasp reality with both hands and go beyond it. I shall not give in to fatigue born of dejection. You help me. You lend me your strength. We innovate. Now and at all times.

Reality

In July 1983, an Arab girl, hardly three months old, died in Paris from the consequences of a clitoridectomy. An operation still possible in France where capital punishment has just been abolished. A crib inundated with blood. A baby girl slaughtered. My likeness, this is reality. Hers and ours. Murdered in your sex, little child, victim of customs, you will not be forgotten.

We think of her. We do not ignore violence. Day after day, we protest patriarchy.

Reality Again

Guelph, Ontario. A shelter for battered women. 9 p.m.
I admit Diana. Diabetes. Both legs amputated.

Battered, she had thrown first her wheelchair, then her-
self, from the front porch of her house. Her twelve-
year-old son had wheeled her to the shelter.

At 10 o'clock, Victoria is admitted. Injured. Lapidated.
Defeated. Escaped with two children.

Violated women. Violated lives. Black horror tinted
with blood. I feel void. Drained. Marred. I can't speak
anymore. I weep.

My daughter, my likeness, do not cry with me. The
indubitable utopia must rise.

Reality III

Woman may not walk alone.

Sunday drivers. Jeering males. An exhibitionist at the entrance to the subway station. Short, meek, clutching a plastic bag. Letting it fall. His open fly exposes what interests only him.

They all feel provoked by the nonchalant steps of woman walking by herself. Imperfect liberation. Yet the essential dream continues.

We take stock. Studiously. We test ourselves. We innovate. Sometimes my beautiful radical one finds her irreducible roots politically incorrect. Together we pursue the difficult identification of women in a language which we attempt to modify. At times we are mute. We stutter, yes, laughingly open-mouthed, delighted when we discern the essential, when infirmity vanishes and voluptuousness rises. Learners at any age, we learn with pleasure and by heart.

The choir of women. Other. Same. Similarly other. Do you hear it, so strong, so melodious?

Transformation. Carefully we walk the road made by double-axed women. We proudly preserve the silver labrys, the symbolic gift of our mothers. Breasts burning from caresses. No more mutilations.

I carry my amazon with me in my personal notes. She gallops afar. Capable rider, I proudly wear the colours of my young mistress. I have become balanced balance. A base no longer shaky. Angry and generous mare. Sensitive, independent mother. Source. Sorceress. Nothing remains hidden, everything is double. Multiple happiness.

In measureless measure every movement is giving and receiving. I measure your heartbeat. I measure your smile. I lose all measure and squander my love.

Belonging is mutual. Infinite. Mother, daughter, same and other forever, gentle in gesture and form.

Distances are meant to be bridged, cords to be tied gently. Nothing is meant to choke, enslave or destroy: punitive terms which must be erased even though it was a woman, Margaret Thatcher, who declared in 1983 that she was going to reestablish the death penalty.

Reality IV

The utopian dream strengthens us. We are no longer divided. Our hearts delight. We say the unsayable. We laugh at what is forbidden.

We do not speak of death. Of suicide. Life is desirable. Utopia is joyous. Its abstraction is our reality. The other reality. The real reality.

Women's arduous dream.

We are approaching its coast. The moment is precious.

I imagine a spacious island of white perfumes and blue delights. Impatience has vanished. Flowers have taken its name. Baltic Mother Sea is in our midst.

A need to write. Blue. To say blue and know by heart the colours of love. Hazy blue heart. At times. Often. A need to stop analyzing, measuring. A desire to go beyond measure. A space, blue and white. Mine. Yours. Ours. Island of being, essential, boundless, you are without measure. Incommensurable island where all distances can be bridged. At all times. When I feel the urge to touch my likeness, my reality, the similarly other, I will be able to do so. No need to stretch in pain. No fear to lose contact with the woman who is ashes.

Yet I want to stretch. Into all contradictions. All pleasurable differences. And at the same time I want to shake off weight and burden. Love without fear in this multi-coloured plenitude of mothers and daughters.

EPILOGUE

I look at you and see myself. You, so different from me and similar. Otherly similar. Still, intimacy is precious. Gone, however, is the need to hang on to each other. Our chains of love have been loosened, yet we are strong enough to hold us safe and free.

We flew to Venice to celebrate our bond. We were happy, at all times, surrounded by water.

In the end, we came back to our different worlds. Living in them separately. Forever aware where to find utopia.

Utopia, the secret place where we exchange energy, a time to look at one another, lovingly.

BY THE SAME AUTHOR

FICTION
Bleu sur blanc: Souvenirs de Tunisie, 2000
(Trillium Award Finalist).
Les Crus de l'Esplanade, 1998
(Trillium Award Finalist).
La Bicyclette, 1997.
La Soupe, 1995
(Grand Prix du Salon du livre de Toronto).
Conversations dans l'Interzone
(in collaboration with Paul Savoie), 1995.
Le Bonheur de la chambre noire, 1993 and 1996.
L'Homme-papier, 1992.
Courts Métrages et Instantanés, 1991.
De mémoire de femme, 1982 and 2002
(Prix du *Journal de Montréal*).

NONFICTION
Paroles rebelles, edited by Marguerite Andersen
and Christine Klein-Lataud, 1992.
Mother Was Not a Person: Writings by Montreal Women,
edited by Marguerite Andersen, 1972 and 1975.
Mécanismes structuraux: Méthode de phonétique corrective
(in collaboration with Huguette Uguay), 1967.
Paul Claudel et l'Allemagne, 1965.

TRANSLATIONS
*Palu, Louie and Charlie Angus, Industrial Cathedrals of the
North/Cathédrales industrielles du Nord*, 1999.

AGMV Marquis

MEMBER OF SCABRINI MEDIA

Quebec, Canada
2003